science QUEST

NATIONAL GEOGRAPHIC   Washington D.C.

Killing Germs, Saving Lives

The Quest for the First Vaccines

Glen Phelan

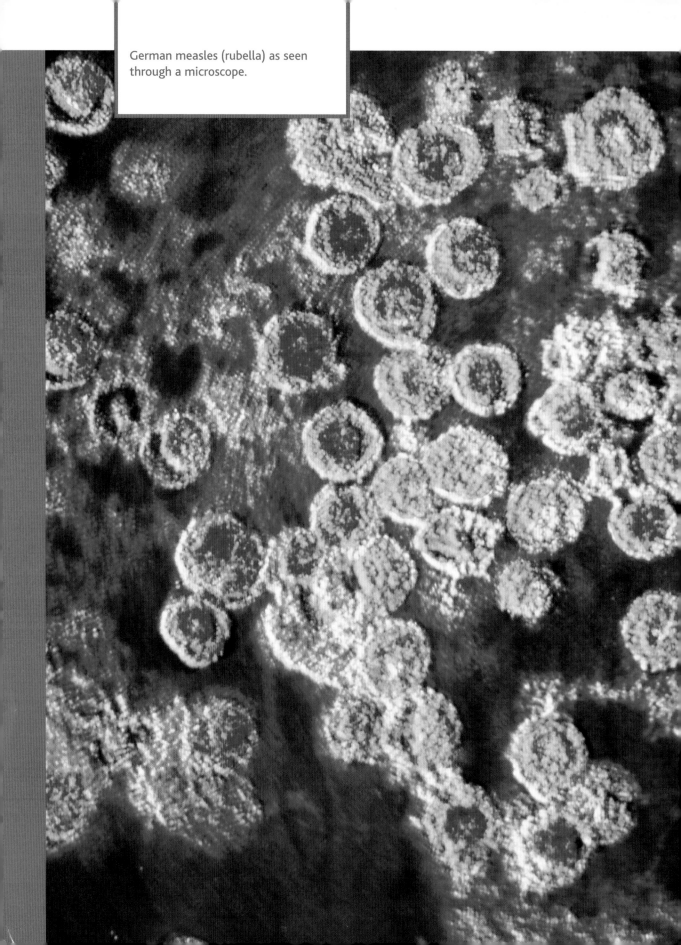

German measles (rubella) as seen through a microscope.

CONTENTS

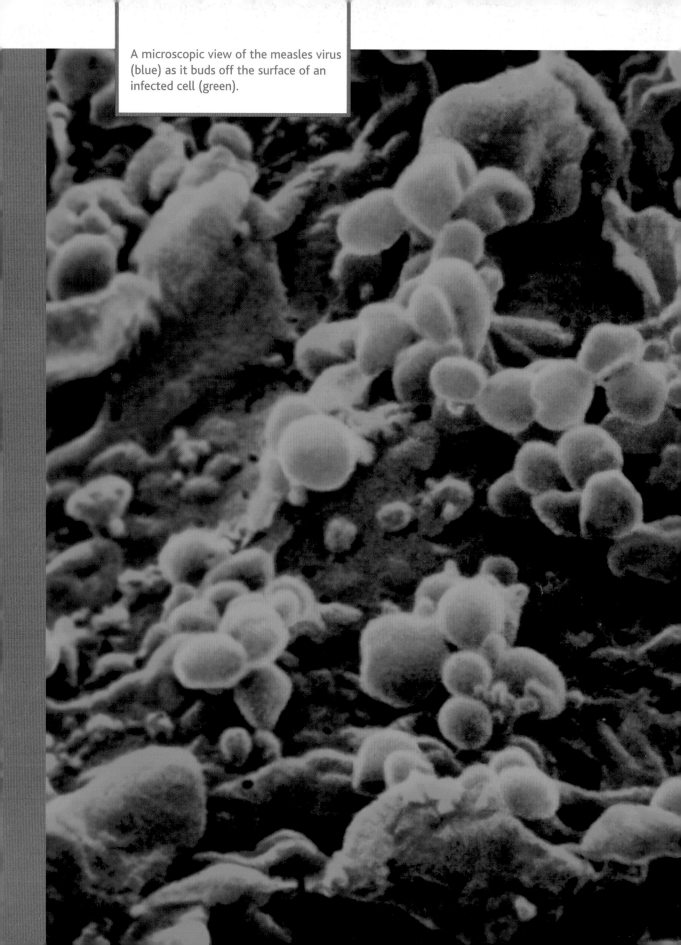

A microscopic view of the measles virus (blue) as it buds off the surface of an infected cell (green).

INTRODUCTION

A "mad dog" causes terror in the streets. Mysterious diseases threaten a nation's economy. Children are struck by deadly illnesses. And no one knows why. This is a story about people who found out why. It's a story about people who fought on the front lines in the first key battles against disease and found something that would change our world forever—vaccines.

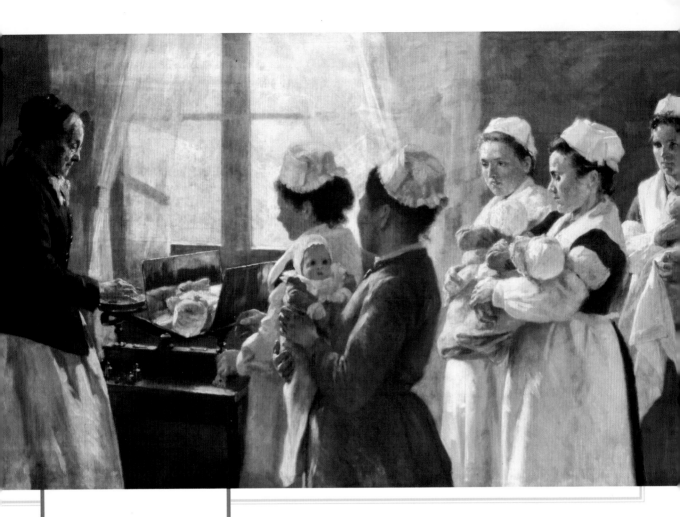

Nurses line up to weigh babies in a hospital in the mid-1800s. Childhood diseases were a constant fear at this time, and their causes were largely unknown.

Generally given as shots, some of the most common vaccines today prevent measles, tetanus, and the flu. Many other diseases, such as smallpox, diptheria, cholera, and polio, have been all but eradicated in much of the world by vaccines.

Who were the heroes responsible for this amazing progress? They were scientists like Louis Pasteur and Robert Koch. These men probed the microscopic world of germs. They were doctors like Joseph Lister and nurses like Florence Nightingale. They worked to make hospital care safer. But what did these people do that was so heroic? Follow their quest and find out.

These men probed
the microscopic
world of germs.

Before Vaccines

By the mid-1800s technology had begun to make the
world a smaller place. The puffs of smoke and the chug-
chug of trains became more common as railroads connect-
ed towns across the countryside. The telephone, invented
in 1876, brought people even closer together. Streetcars
and elevators made life easier in cities. And electric light
bulbs changed life forever. Every year seemed to bring
new developments in science and technology.

Progress was being made in medicine, too, but not fast
enough. If you were a sick child in the mid-1800s, there
was plenty of reason for your parents to worry. Diseases,
including everyday ailments such as the flu, strep throat,
and the measles, were killers. Epidemics killed thousands
of people who were defenseless against the spread
of disease. No one knew what caused diseases, how they
spread, or how to treat them.

People had some theories, of course. Many thought diseases
were spread by poisonous vapors from swamps, animal
wastes, and decaying matter. These things seemed unhealthy,
so the idea made sense. But there was no scientific proof to
support this idea. No one understood the causes of diseases.
So they didn't know how to protect themselves.

science BOOSTER

What Is a Vaccine?

A vaccine is a medical prevention tool. Technically, it is a
preparation of dead or weakened microorganisms that
helps the body provide immunity from disease. In less con-
fusing terms, a vaccine intro-
duces a very weak version of
the disease, or antigen, to the
body. When the body recog-
nizes the antigen as foreign, it
fights off the disease. Because
your body is designed to
"remember" germs, the vaccination procedure prevents you
from getting infected with a
more serious occurrence of
the same disease should the
germs enter your body later.

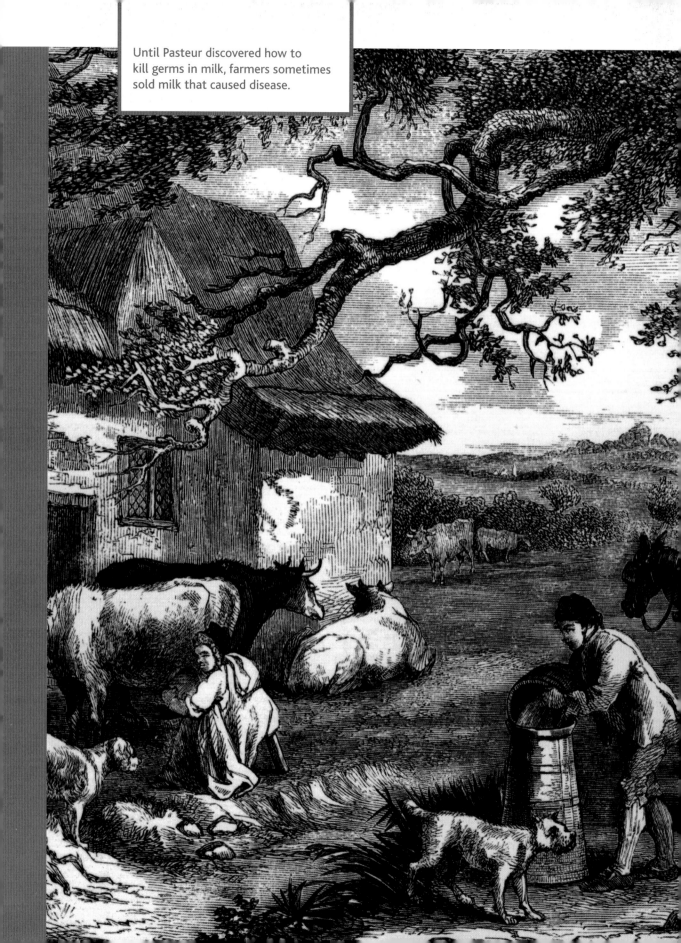

Until Pasteur discovered how to kill germs in milk, farmers sometimes sold milk that caused disease.

THE EARLY DAYS

At the end of the 18th century, in 1796, an English doctor named Edward Jenner had made a most auspicious discovery. He had discovered a way to prevent the deadly disease called smallpox.

Edward Jenner

BORN May 17, 1749
Berkeley, England

DIED January 26, 1823
Berkeley, England

Edward Jenner began studying with a local surgeon at the age of 13. At 21, he went to study in London. There, a teacher taught him to always test his ideas with experiments. Later, Jenner served as a surgeon in the British army.

All of these experiences led him to his greatest discovery. He developed a vaccine made from cowpox pus that protected people who received it against smallpox. This is the first recorded vaccine in history.

Later, Jenner returned to the countryside where he was born and became a doctor. He practiced medicine there for the rest of his life.

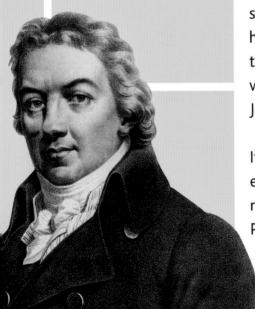

1776 The U.S. Declaration of Independence is signed.

1749 Edward Jenner is born.

1789 The French Revolution begins

Jenner noticed what many farmers in his village knew: People who milked cows sometimes got cowpox, a mild and fairly harmless form of smallpox. He also noticed that people who had gotten cowpox almost never got smallpox. It seemed that cowpox gave a person immunity, or protection, from smallpox.

After a lot of study, Jenner tested this idea. He rubbed pus from a cowpox sore into a scratch made in the arm of a healthy boy. The boy got cowpox as expected. Then about six weeks later Jenner placed pus from a smallpox sore into the boy's arm. And just as he'd hoped, nothing happened. The boy did not get smallpox. Jenner had created the first safe vaccine. Soon, people were getting vaccinated with cowpox so they would not get smallpox later on. But Jenner did not fully understand why his vaccine worked.

It would take the continued work of other scientists to eventually learn how this was possible. Armed with a microscope and a few other tools, a scientist named Louis Pasteur took up the quest.

1796

Jenner creates
smallpox vaccine.

This painting by French artist
Claude Monet, *Train in the
Country*, shows a common
scene in mid-1800s France.

A Hero of His Time

One day in 1831, a wolf wandered out of the woods near
a French village. The wolf was foaming at the mouth. It had
a deadly disease called rabies. The wolf bit several people.
Now they would get rabies, too.

The victims went to the village blacksmith to have their
wounds burned. The shop was near the home of eight-
year-old Louis Pasteur. He never forgot the screams of
pain he heard that day.

Born in 1822, young Louis Pasteur faced many challenges.
At that time, deadly diseases often struck infants and
children. In fact, Louis's older brother had died as an infant.
But Louis grew up healthy and happy.

It seemed that
cowpox gave a
person immunity,
or protection,
from smallpox.

The École Normale in Paris, France, which Pasteur attended.

After graduating from college, where he studied chemistry and physics, Louis became a professor. In addition to his teaching, he worked long hours in his laboratory. But even with all this work, he did find time to fall in love with a woman named Marie Laurent. They were married, and his new wife was a great help in his work.

The work of Louis Pasteur was greatly influenced by the world he encountered. Not only did his experience as a child motivate him to study disease, but so did his life experiences as an adult.

Louis Pasteur

BORN December 27, 1822
Dole, France

DIED September 28, 1895
Saint-Cloud, France

Growing up in the town of Arbois in Eastern France, Louis enjoyed swimming and fishing, but his favorite pastime was art. He loved to draw and paint and had a good eye for detail. He would study his subject carefully, whether it was a flower, a butterfly, or a face. Then he would capture every detail in his artwork.

Louis was just as careful in his schoolwork. He worked slowly and carefully, checking and re-checking his work until he thought it was good enough to hand in. His strong powers of observation and careful attention to detail would be important skills later in his scientific work.

Curiosity was another of young Louis Pasteur's traits. He was always asking questions. Louis loved sharing knowledge as much as learning it. He decided to become a teacher—the best one possible.

After graduating from a prep school, Louis studied hard to prepare to take the entrance exam to the École Normale. This was a famous school in Paris that trained people to become professors. Only those who had top scores on the exam were admitted to the École Normale. Louis was excited about the challenge.

Then a strange thing happened. Louis was accepted into the school, but he turned down the offer! Why? Only 22 students were accepted from all of France. But Louis had placed 15th on the list. He thought he could do a lot better than that. So he decided to study one more year then take the test again. When Louis took the test again, he placed 4th. That was good enough for him. He entered the École Normale in Paris.

Later, he studied chemistry at the Sorbonne in Paris. He went on to become a teacher and researcher.

Pasteur has been called the greatest contributor to medical science of the 19th century. He proved that microorganisms cause disease. He saved the alcohol, wine, and silk industries of France. He also developed the process of pasteurization, using heat to kill germs in food. And he discovered how to make vaccines, which helped prevent diseases such as anthrax, chicken cholera, and rabies.

1820 | Florence Nightingale is born.

1822 | Louis Pasteur is born.

After ten years of marriage, the Pasteurs were very busy with work and a family of four children. Then tragedy struck. One day while visiting her grandfather, the Pasteur's oldest daughter, Jeanne, became ill with typhoid fever. In the 1850s, no one knew what caused this common disease, how to prevent it, or how to treat it. Little Jeanne died. It was a tragedy that many families suffered. The Pasteurs would have more than their share.

Pasteur made many discoveries that would help prevent infectious diseases like the one that killed Jeanne. The first of these discoveries was what he called "wee germs." Using a microscope (a new tool at the time), Pasteur discovered that liquids such as milk and fruit juice contain tiny living things. Some of these "wee germs" made the liquid spoil.

Pasteur discovered that he could kill the harmful germs by heating the liquid to certain temperatures. This process became known as pasteurization.

Silkworms, shown on a mulberry plant, were essential to the French clothing industry.

Pasteurization made food safe. It made milk last longer before spoiling. It also killed harmful germs in milk that caused some diseases, though Pasteur did not yet know that germs caused disease. Pasteurization results would change medicine forever. It is still used today to destroy germs in milk, cheese, and other foods.

In 1865, Pasteur was asked to look into another problem. A mysterious disease was killing silkworms throughout France. Silkworms spin cocoons made of silk fibers. The fibers are woven into silk cloth. Without silk, the French clothing industry was in big trouble.

1823

Edward Jenner dies.

1827

Joseph Lister is born.

1843

Robert Koch is born.

At first, Pasteur knew nothing about silkworms. But he learned everything he could about them. Pasteur used his microscope to observe healthy and sick worms. He saw oval shapes on the sick worms. He guessed that these shapes were germs that caused a disease in the worms. After a lot more observation and research, Pasteur knew that he was right.

To solve the silkworm problem, the diseased silkworms had to be found and destroyed. Pasteur taught the silkworm growers how to use microscopes. Then they could identify the germs in the silkworms or in the moths they turned into. If the germs were found, the worms, the moths, or any eggs the moths had laid were destroyed. In this way, only healthy silkworms were allowed to grow.

Then the problem became more difficult. Some of the worms in the population that no longer had the disease got sick. After many more long days in his lab, Pasteur found that a different kind of germ was causing another silkworm disease. He showed growers how to control the spread of both diseases.

science BOOSTER

Ghost Germs
In the 1860s, Pasteur made another important discovery. He proved that germs come only from other germs. That sounds pretty simple. However, many people believed that microorganisms were created suddenly from nonliving matter, like air and mud. In a simple experiment, Pasteur showed that germs do not appear "out of thin air."

The U.S annexes Texas.

Louis Pasteur with his daughter Camille

Success—and Sorrow

Pasteur had saved the clothing industry in France. He was hailed as a national hero. But in the midst of this success, the Pasteur family suffered great sorrow. In September 1865, their youngest daughter, two-year-old Camille, became ill. She died of typhoid fever a few months later.

About eight months after that, the Pasteurs' 12-year-old daughter, Cecile, also caught typhoid fever and died. Three of the Pasteur children had now died from an infectious disease that doctors were powerless to cure.

The stress of his children's deaths and his constant work took their toll on Pasteur. In 1868, he suffered a stroke and nearly died. He recovered, but he was never again able to speak, walk, or use his hands as well as he once did. Still, his most important work lay ahead.

> To solve the silkworm problem, the diseased silkworms had to be found and destroyed.

The Prussians used the Hall of Mirrors in the Palace of Versailles as a military hospital.

ON THE FRONT LINES

In 1870, war broke out between France and Prussia, a German state. The powerful Prussian army crushed the French defenses and marched to Paris. France lost the war. The defeat was heartbreaking to Pasteur. Even more heartbreaking were the thousands of wounded soldiers who filled the hospitals and clinics of Paris.

1849

Louis Pasteur gets married.

1861–1865

U.S. Civil War.

1854

Crimean War in Russia.

The soldiers were suffering from more than bullet wounds. Many soldiers grew sick because their wounds became infected. That means that germs had gotten into the wounds and were multiplying enough to cause disease.

At that time, however, people still believed diseases were caused by poisonous vapors in the air. They thought that the wind blew this unhealthy air all over the place and caused diseases. Pasteur's work over the years, however, was pointing to the fact that diseases were probably caused by germs. Yet germs couldn't travel from person to person by themselves.

Pasteur thought that doctors often spread diseases. He studied samples of infected flesh from the wounds of the soldiers in Paris. Under the microscope, he saw what he expected. The samples from the wounds were full of germs. Pasteur was certain that doctors were spreading the germs as they went from patient to patient.

> If you were lucky enough to survive a surgery, there was a good chance an infection would kill you afterward.

In the Franco-Prussian War, the French suffered a terrible defeat.

Dirty Surgery

Most hospitals back then were dirty places. Surgeons operated in their street clothes. They didn't wear gloves or masks. They often didn't even wash their hands or instruments as they treated different patients. If you were lucky enough to survive an operation, there was a good chance an infection would kill you afterward. Most doctors doubted Pasteur's idea that they were spreading disease. But a Scottish surgeon named Joseph Lister knew that Pasteur was right.

Joseph Lister

BORN April 5, 1827
Essex, England

DIED February 10, 1912
Walmer, England

Joseph Lister's father taught him to use a microscope. He attended Quaker schools as a child and studied at University College in London. He studied arts and medicine at the same time. Lister was a very good student and graduated with honors.

Lister went on to become a surgeon and researcher. He was the first person to make sure the area around a patient having surgery was kept clean. He based this practice on the idea that bacteria should never be allowed to enter a wound. Lister's work led to the widespread use of antiseptics in hospitals. He made surgery a safer process.

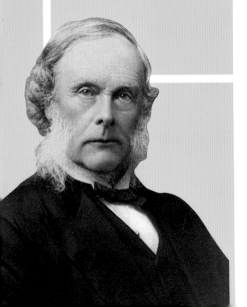

1865 Lister uses anticeptic to kill germs in surgery.

1869 United States' transcontinental railroad is completed.

1870–1871 Franco-Prussian

Over the years, Lister had read Pasteur's reports about germs. Pasteur's work convinced Lister that his surgical patients were becoming infected not from the air but from germs *in* the air.

Lister thought of a way to keep germs out of the patient during surgery. He soaked bandages with an antiseptic called carbolic acid. This chemical killed germs. He surrounded the surgical wound with these bandages to keep germs out. Then he washed his hands and surgical instruments with carbolic acid. Finally, he sprayed a fine mist of carbolic acid over the patient during the operation.

Lister's results were amazing. Previously, about 45 percent of his patients had died from infections after an operation. Now, he had cut that number to 15 percent.

Need Surgery?

Sometimes when people get sick they need to have surgery. Having surgery is never without risks, but it was sure a lot less safe in the past than it is now. It used to be that tools weren't even sterilized between use on patients! Today doctors and nurses are very conscious of protecting both the patients and themselves from spreading germs.

One thing that hasn't changed very much over the years though is the actual tools. Many of the tools used today in surgery were just a little more crude back in the days of Louis Pasteur, but otherwise very similar. Take a look at this naval surgery set from the early 1900s which shows some tools that were used. But don't be fooled—the tools may be the same today, but they're a lot cleaner!

When would you rather have been a patient needing surgery?

1 Forceps – to grasp or create traction on something

2 Bone saw – for amputation

3 Scarifier – to create small holes or scratches in the skin

4 Tooth wrench – to help with tooth removal

5 6 7 13 Parts of a catheter set – to keep small passages open

8 9 Amputation knives

10 11 Clippers – for snipping bone

12 Mirror

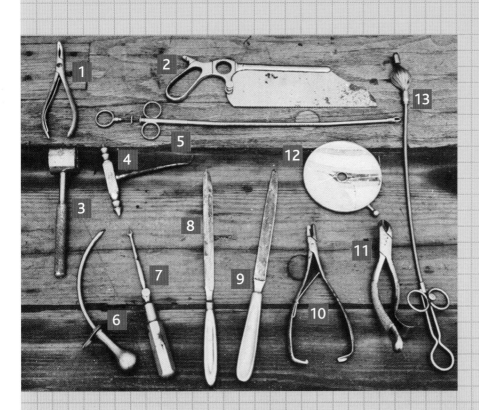

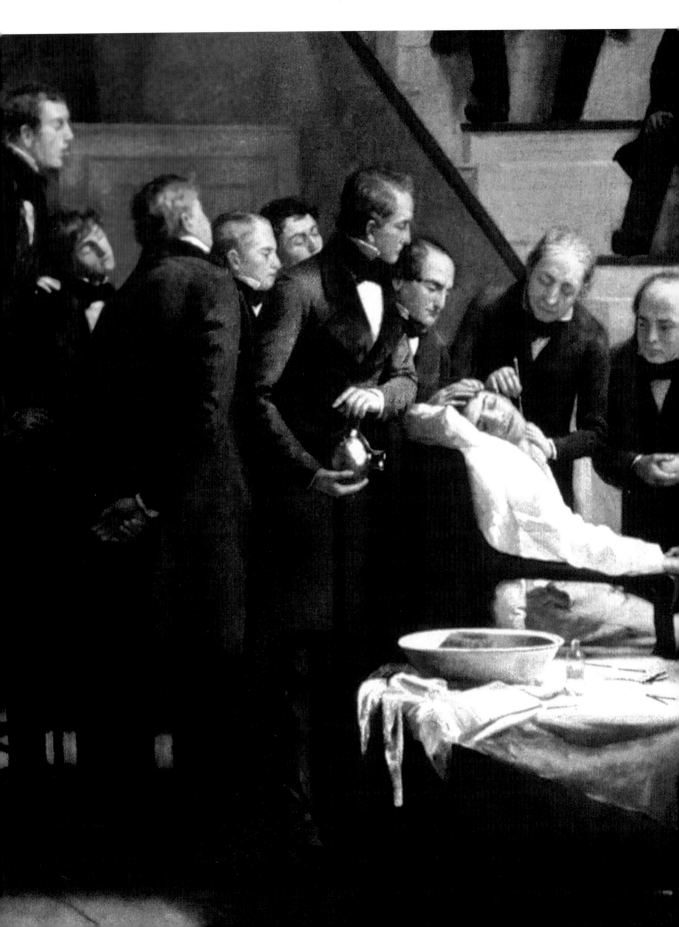

A team of surgeons operates on a patient at Massachusetts General Hospital in Boston in 1846.

A painting of Florence Nightingale in a hospital ward

Modern Nursing Is Born

Lister's methods were even more successful when they were combined with the ideas of Florence Nightingale, a nurse who'd served in the war. During the Crimean War in Russia in 1854, the British government asked Nightingale to run an army hospital. The hospital was filthy and low on supplies. But Nightingale turned things around with her new ideas. In just a few months, the death rate fell from about 40 percent to only 2 percent.

1870

15th amendment to the United States Constitution is passed giving the right to vote to all citizens.

1870s

Germ theory of disease gains acceptance.

Florence Nightingale

BORN May 12, 1820
Florence, Italy

DIED August 13, 1910
London, England

Born into a wealthy family, Nightingale could have lived a life of luxury. Instead she chose to devote her life to helping others. When she was 30 years old, she began training as a nurse.

After the Crimean War, her fame spread around the world. The United States asked her advice about setting up army hospitals during the Civil War. She set up a nursing school in London. There she trained her nurses to provide the best scientific care possible. Soon her nurses were working in such faraway places as Australia and India.

Nightingale founded the profession of trained nursing and advised governments worldwide on scientific care for the sick. Her work led to safer hospitals around the world.

After the war, Nightingale was welcomed home as a hero. She used her reputation to improve hospital care throughout England. She said that hospitals should be kept clean. The rooms should have plenty of space and large windows to let fresh air circulate.

Nightingale thought all of this would keep the air free of poisonous vapors. Although she didn't know about germs then, her ideas did reduce the number of germs in hospitals. Hospitals became healthier places.

While Lister and Nightingale were working to keep hospitals free of germs, Pasteur continued to study the connection between germs and disease. But he wasn't the only one. In Germany, Robert Koch, a doctor, also had been busy peering through his microscope.

Robert Koch

BORN December 11, 1843
Klausthal, Germany

DIED May 27, 1910
Baden-Baden, Germany

In many ways, Robert Koch's life was similar to that of Pasteur. Koch grew up in a small town near forested mountains. He loved exploring nature and listening to his father's stories, as Pasteur had. Both men were fascinated by creatures that could be seen only with a microscope.

Koch became a doctor famous for studying bacteria. He was the first to show that specific bacteria cause specific diseases. In 1872, Koch began to study anthrax, a disease that killed farm animals. He discovered the bacterium that causes it and described the steps to help other scientists study bacteria. Like Pasteur, Koch developed methods of immunizing people against disease.

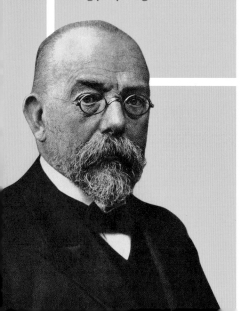

1874

First Impressionist exhibition of art is held in Paris, France.

1876

Telephone is invented.

Koch read about the work of Pasteur and became inspired to conduct his own research on germs. In the 1870s, both scientists concluded that germs cause infectious diseases and that specific germs cause specific diseases. These conclusions are called the germ theory of disease.

Koch worked out a way of showing which kind of germ causes a certain disease. In 1876, he used this method to discover the germ—a certain kind of bacterium—that causes anthrax in livestock. This disease, deadly to cattle and sheep, also could spread to humans.

More than anyone else, Pasteur recognized the importance of this discovery. Now scientists could start to identify the germs that cause disease in people and animals. Then maybe, just maybe, they would be able to cure or prevent infectious diseases.

In his lab, Robert Koch looks through a microscope for germs that cause illness.

Farm diseases gave Jenner the idea
of how to make a vaccine.

THE FIRST VACCINES

In 1879, an epidemic was sweeping through the barnyards of France. A disease called chicken cholera was killing nine out of every ten chickens it infected. Once again, it was Pasteur to the rescue! This time he had a new weapon to fight the mysterious disease—the germ theory. As in many scientific discoveries, luck would also play a part.

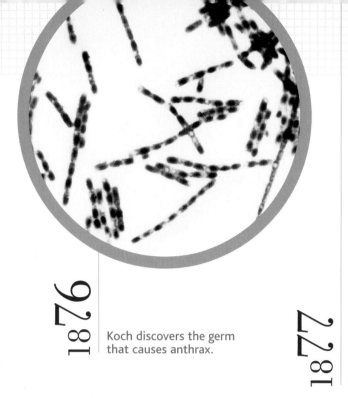

1876 Koch discovers the germ that causes anthrax.

1877 Koch publishes rules to test germs as causes for specific diseases.

1879 Cholera hits France, killing nine out of ten infected chickens.

Other scientists had already found out what germ causes chicken cholera. Pasteur began growing these germs. By experimenting with the germs, he hoped to answer these questions: Can the germs be made weaker? Can the weakened germs be used to fight the disease?

Pasteur began thinking back on the work of Edward Jenner, the English doctor who had created a smallpox vaccine more than 80 years earlier. Although Jenner did not know why his vaccine worked, Pasteur could see from Jenner's results that the weakened germs of a disease could somehow protect the body against the stronger form. But he didn't know how to weaken the germs. The answer came by accident.

Pasteur took a summer vacation. He left cultures of chicken cholera germs with his lab assistants. But they took a vacation, too, and left the cultures unattended.

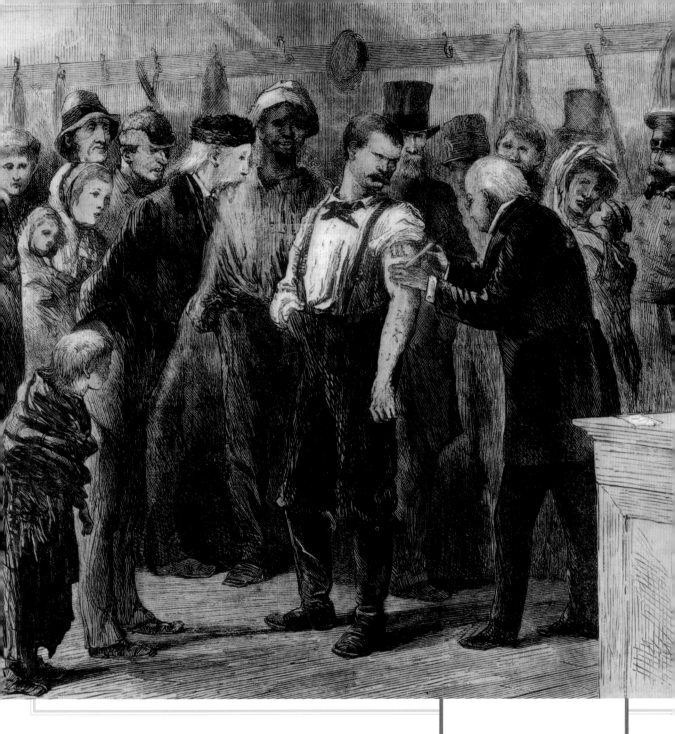

A cartoon shows people lining up to receive cowpox vaccines from Jenner.

When Pasteur returned, the cultures of cholera germs were mostly dried out. His lab assistants were going to throw them away. Then they had a better idea. Why not see how powerful these germs were? Pasteur injected the germs that were still alive into some chickens.

1881

Pasteur makes anthrax vaccine.

1885

Pasteur vaccinates
Joseph Meister for rabies.

> Livestock all
> around the world
> were protected
> from anthrax.

The chickens did not get sick. Apparently the germs were too weak to cause the disease. Then Pasteur injected the same chickens, as well as some new chickens, with a strong dose of the germs. The new chickens got sick. But to everyone's amazement, the chickens that had received the first dose of weak germs stayed healthy.

Pasteur and his assistants had made a chicken cholera vaccine by drying germs in the open air. Pasteur started using this method to find vaccines for other diseases.

By 1881, Pasteur had made an anthrax vaccine using the germ that Robert Koch had shown to cause anthrax. He tested it on sheep at a farm outside Paris. The vaccinated animals survived when given anthrax germs. Pasteur began making and selling his vaccine to farmers and to veterinarians. Soon, livestock all around the world were protected from anthrax.

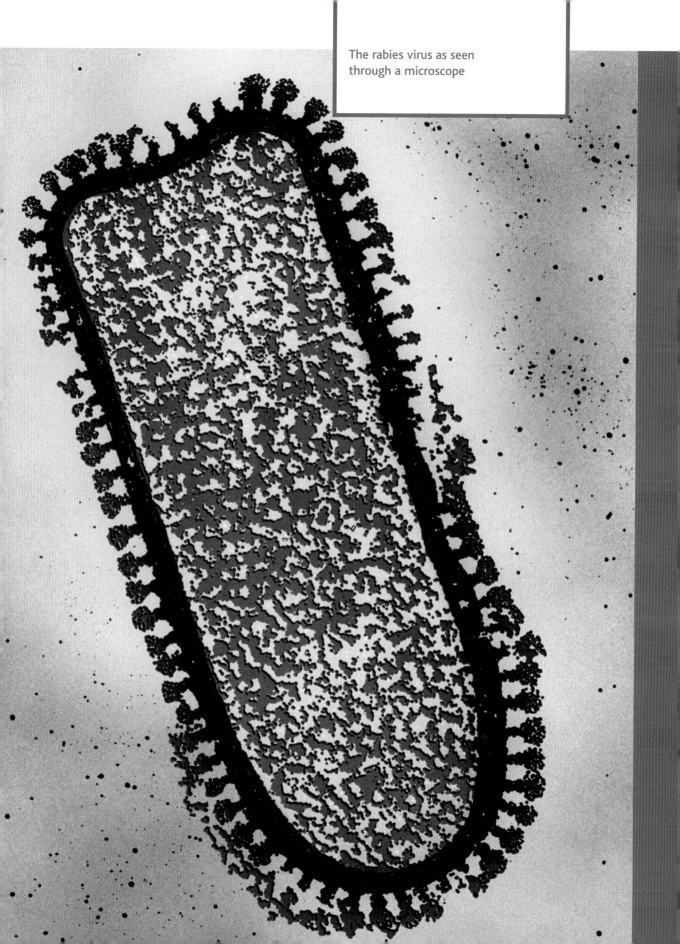

The rabies virus as seen through a microscope

Joseph Meister grew up near this
village in the Alsace region of France.

A QUEST FULFILLED

July 4, 1885, was a terrible day for nine-year-old Joseph Meister. On that day, he was attacked by a dog with rabies. There was no cure for rabies. But the doctor in his village had heard of a man who was experimenting with a new treatment. It was the boy's only hope. "Go to Paris," the doctor told Joseph's mother. "Go to Louis Pasteur!"

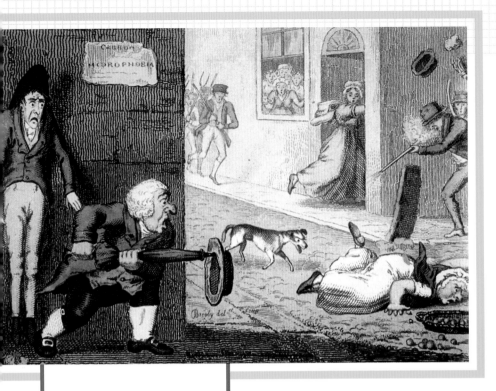

1888

Pasteur Institute is established in Paris.

Cartoon of a "mad dog" causing panic on a London street

Pasteur had learned a lot about vaccines in his work on animal diseases. But more and more he was turning his attention to making vaccines for human diseases.

The first human disease he studied was rabies. People got rabies from the bite of an infected animal. Rabies was fairly rare. But the thought of a rabid "mad dog" prowling the streets and attacking people was terrifying to everyone.

Pasteur still remembered that day long ago when a rabid wolf had attacked villages near his home. The painful treatment, which included burning the wounds, didn't work. But no one had come up with a better idea.

Pasteur knew that the first step in finding a rabies vaccine was to find the rabies germ. He spent long hours looking through his microscope. He looked at the blood of infected animals. He looked at their saliva. He couldn't find the germs. Why not?

Another Kind of Germ

Pasteur didn't know that the germ that causes rabies is a virus. It was too small to be seen with the microscopes available in the 1800s. The other diseases Pasteur had studied are caused by bacteria. They were large enough to be seen with his microscopes.

Pasteur knew that rabies attacks the nervous system. So he reasoned that the germs must be in the brain and spinal cord. He took the spinal cords of rabbits that had died from rabies, and dried them in bottles for 14 days. This made the germs in the cords almost harmless. Pasteur used the cords to make the first rabies vaccine.

Pasteur found that the best way to give a vaccine was in a series of shots. The first shot contained the weakest germs. The next shots contained slightly stronger germs. In this way the body gradually built up defenses against the disease.

> The thought of a rabid "mad dog" prowling the streets and attacking people was terrifying to everyone.

Diseases made preventable by vaccines

Today, there are many diseases that can be prevented by vaccines. These are among the diseases that are most commonly vaccinated against.

Measles

One of the most contagious diseases known, measles is caused by the measles virus and causes rashes and fever. Measles is usually spread through contact with an infected person.

Tetanus

This disease is usually caused by exposure to bacteria carrying the disease spores. It is not transmitted from person to person but can develop from germs caught in a wound or cut.

Mumps

Generally a childhood disease, mumps is an infection caused by a virus. It usually affects the salivary glands and is spread through contact with an infected person.

Chickenpox

A disease that is spread very easily and is most common in children under 15 years old. Although a mild sickness, chickenpox is very uncomfortable and can cause more serious problems in later life. This illness usually shows up as bumps or sores on the person's body.

Tuberculosis (TB)

TB is a disease that affects the lungs or other parts of the body, such as the bones, joints, or brain. Not everyone infected with TB bacteria actually develops the disease. TB can be spread through the air like the flu.

Most people in the United States receive vaccinations for the diseases mentioned above, among others, during childhood. It is important to know that some people can't be vaccinated for medical reasons, while others may not receive vaccinations because of their families' beliefs.

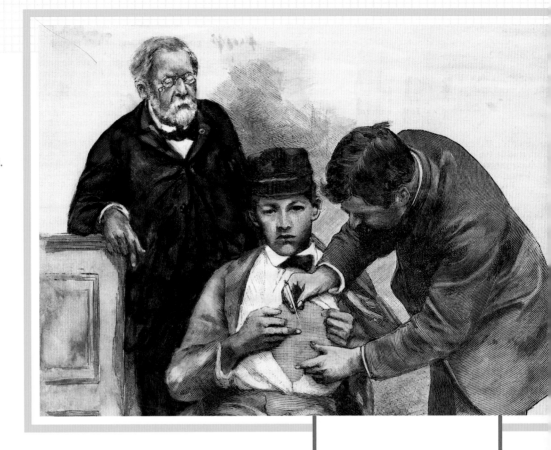

This 1885 illustration from *Scientific American* shows Pasteur looking on as an assistant vaccinates Joseph Meister.

By July of 1885, Pasteur had vaccinated 50 dogs with great results. But no human had been successfully vaccinated. That's when Joseph Meister walked into the lab. Pasteur now faced the toughest decision of his life. He was certain the vaccine could protect someone before the person was bitten. But could it fight the infection after someone was bitten? He didn't know. What if it made the infection worse? Doctors assured Pasteur that Joseph would certainly die without treatment. There was no time to delay. Pasteur gave Joseph a series of shots over the next 10 days. Then he waited, and he worried.

The days passed into weeks, the weeks into months. Joseph stayed healthy. He never got rabies. Pasteur had done it! He had made a rabies vaccine. The world now had a way to fight this terrible disease.

A laboratory inside the
Pasteur Institute in France.

THE WORK CONTINUES

5

The news of the rabies vaccine spread. Soon rabies victims from all over Europe came to Paris to be vaccinated. Four boys from New Jersey even made a trip across the Atlantic Ocean. It was a trip that saved their lives. Louis Pasteur was a hero not only in France but around the world.

Patients from different nations wait outside the Pasteur Institute in Paris in the 1890s.

The success of the rabies vaccine made people realize that many other diseases could be cured or prevented. People and governments from around the world sent money to build a research laboratory in Paris. In 1888, the Pasteur Institute opened its doors with Louis Pasteur as its director.

Pasteur suffered another stroke in 1887, leaving him unable to do much research himself. However, many other scientists carried on the work that Pasteur had started. Over the years, the Pasteur Institute set up branches all over the world. Its scientists discovered the causes of many other infectious diseases and developed vaccines for them, too.

1924

Vaccine for tetanus is used
in humans for the first time.

1939-1945
World War II

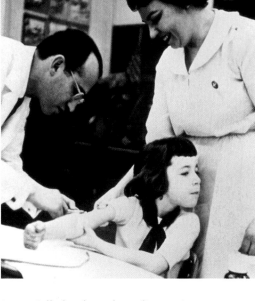

1954
Jonas Salk develops the polio vaccine.

Vaccination Research Takes Off

Breakthroughs at other research labs led to vaccines for
measles, types of flu, and many other diseases. A vaccine
was also found for typhoid fever, the disease that had
killed three of Pasteur's children.

In the 1950s, two American scientists developed vaccines
for polio. Polio was one of the most feared diseases of the
mid-20th century. It seldom killed, but it left people crip-
pled or paralyzed. Summertime, when the disease spread
most rapidly, was an especially anxious time.

In 1954, Jonas Salk developed a polio vaccine. It was given
as a shot. Several years later, Albert Sabin developed a polio
vaccine that people could drink. The Sabin vaccine was also
more powerful than Salk's. Both vaccines were used to stop
polio throughout much of the world. Today, there are fewer
than 800 reported polio cases in the world each year.

In 1888, the
Pasteur Institute
opened its doors.

1964

Vaccine for measles is used in humans for the first time.

1969

First moon walk.

> Each day, new breakthroughs help scientists learn about the potential to save millions of lives through vaccines.

Building on the Past

All of these medical successes built on the work of Louis Pasteur, Robert Koch, and others. When Pasteur developed the vaccine for chicken cholera, some people downplayed his efforts by calling it an accident. Pasteur responded, "Chance favors the prepared mind." He meant that a thoughtful person is prepared to respond in new ways when unexpected opportunities arise. So, for example, when an accident happens, you understand the importance of it.

When Pasteur and his lab assistants saw the dried-out cholera cultures, they didn't throw them away. They understood that the cultures might help answer a question. If they had thrown out those cultures, who knows how many more years it would have taken to make vaccines?

Louis Pasteur changed the way we think about disease. He helped us understand the basic cause of disease. Most important, he helped replace fear with hope. Pasteur, Robert Koch, and other medical researchers showed us that diseases can be conquered.

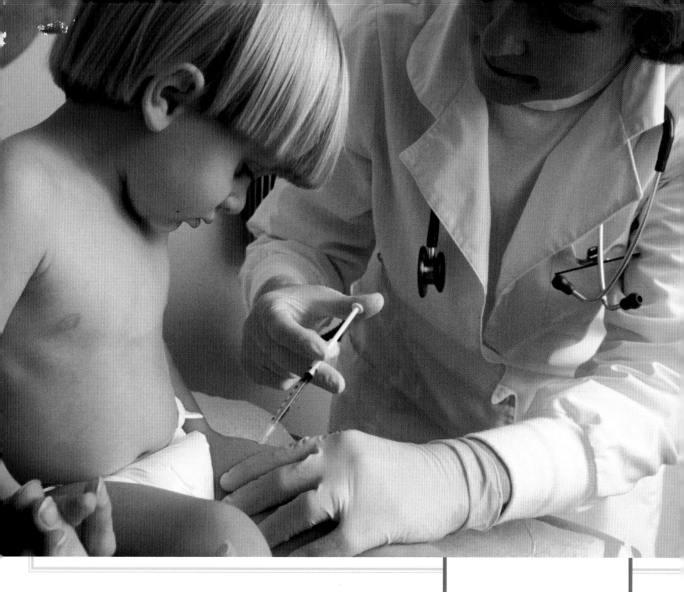

Today, researchers at the Pasteur Institute and other vaccine research centers are experimenting with vaccines for everything from cancer and allergies to malaria and AIDS. Each day, new breakthroughs help scientists learn about the potential to save millions of lives through vaccines. These scientists are curious and dedicated, just like Pasteur.

Like in days past, developing a usable vaccine is very difficult. With the need for animal studies, human studies, and development of the formula, among other complicated steps, it can take more then ten years to develop a proper vaccine.

1977

Smallpox is eradicated worldwide.

1995

Chicken pox vaccine is licensed for use.

Polio Vaccine Developed

33 USA

1999

1979

Last outbreak of the polio virus in the U.S.

The United States Postal Service created a stamp in 1999 to commemorate Jonas Salk and his discovery of the polio vaccine.

Many new vaccines are already at advanced stages of development, including ones that target diseases such as rotavirus, cervical cancer, and meningitis. Already, most people around the world receive vaccination against measles, polio, tetanus, and several other preventable diseases.

Even as world health improves, populations continue to grow and new diseases creep to the forefront. There is a continued need for further research and development in the field of vaccines. April 12, 2005, marked the 50th anniversary of the first polio vaccine.—Just think what might be accomplished in another 50 years!

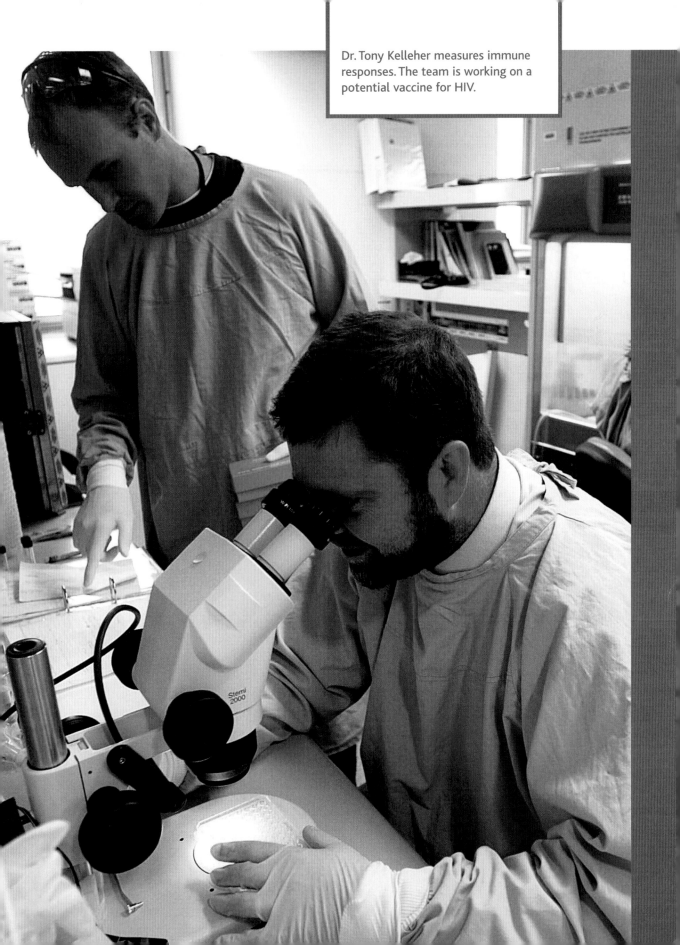

Dr. Tony Kelleher measures immune responses. The team is working on a potential vaccine for HIV.

A petri dish with bacteria cultures as seen through a microscope.

GLOSSARY

Antigen
a weakened version of
a disease that creates an
immune response

Antiseptic
substance that kills
germs and prevents infection

Bacterium
smallest and simplest of all
one-celled organisms. Some
bacteria (plural) cause disease.

Cultures
living material grown
in laboratory dishes

Germ
microorganism that
can cause a disease

**Germ theory
of disease**
idea that infections
and other diseases result
from the action
of microorganisms

Immunity
ability of the body
to defend itself against
disease

Infectious disease
disease that can spread
rapidly from one organism
to another

Pasteurization
process of destroying
unwanted organisms
using heat

Polio
disease, caused by a
virus, that leads to fever
and paralysis

Rabies
disease, caused by a
virus, that leads to paralysis
and death

Smallpox
disease, caused by a
virus, that leads to fever, skin
sores, and often death

Vaccine
preparation of dead or
weakened microorganisms
that prompts the body to
provide immunity from disease

Virus
tiny, disease-causing
structure that can only
reproduce inside a living cell

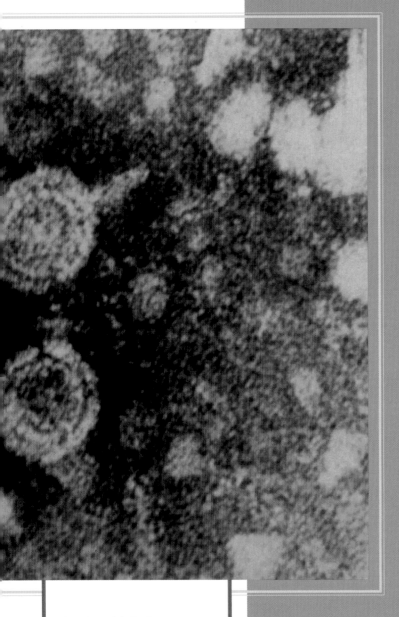

The Hepatitis B virus as seen through a microscope.

Biographical Resources

For more information on Edward Jenner and his scientific studies, go to the Jenner Museum web site at www.jennermuseum.com. They even have games!

To read more about Louis Pasteur and the Pasteur Institute, go to the Pasteur Institute's web site at www.pasteur.fr/english.html.

Would you like to read the original report of Louis Pasteur to the French Academy of Sciences? Head to www.foundersofscience.net/Rabies.htm.

If you'd like to know more about Florence Nightingale, check out the following web sites:

For biographical information, see the BBC at www.bbc.co.uk/history/discovery/medicine/nightingale_01.shtml.

Want to actually hear Florence Nightingale? Go to www.bbc.co.uk/history/multimedia_zone/audio_video/audio/publish/pages/nightingale.shtml to hear an audio clip of her in 1890!

How about reading letters she wrote? Go to http://clendening.kumc.edu/dc/fn/.

To find out more on the scientist Jonas Salk, go to www.salk.edu/jonassalk/.

For more biographical information on scientist Robert Koch head to the Nobel Prize web site at http://nobelprize.org/medicine/laureates/1905/koch-bio.html.

Other cool science stuff about vaccines

The World Health Organization is a great primary source for information on vaccines. See their site at www.who.int/topics/vaccines/en/.

Visit the Sabin Vaccine Institute's web site at www.sabin.org/vaccine.htm.

See the Centers for Disease Control and Prevention's Vaccines and Immunizations page at www.cdc.gov/node.do/id/0900f3ec8000e2f3.

For information on the polio vaccine, go to the CBC's 50th anniversary web site at www.cdc.gov/nip/events/polio-vacc-50th/default.htm.

Wonder how they've been successful in protecting against polio? Go to the Smithsonian National Museum of American History site, "Whatever Happened To Polio?" at http://americanhistory.si.edu/polio/.

Some bacteria can be very nasty. Learn about their cell structure at Cells Alive! www.cellsalive.com/cells/bactcell.htm.

What more can I do?

If you're a teenager or an adult, you may need vaccines too. To find out, visit the CDCs "What Vaccines Do You Need?" web page at www2.cdc.gov/nip/adultImmSched/.

For a cool global web site made just for young people so you discuss and take action on issues that affect you, visit the UNICEF Voices of Youth web site at www.unicef.org/voy/.

Still have questions? Go to the U.S. Department of Energy's "Ask A Scientist" web page at http://newton.dep.anl.gov/aasquesv.htm.

Also, try heading out to your local science museum for more information and fun facts.

RESOURCES

INDEX

Copyright © 2006
National Geographic Society

Published by the National
Geographic Society.

Large parts of this book were previously
published as *Finding the First Vaccines*
(National Geographic Reading
Expeditions), copyright © 2003.

Book design by KINETIK. The body
text of the book is set in Bliss Regular.
The display text is set in Filosofia.

Library of Congress
Cataloging-in-Publication Data

Phelan, Glen.
Killing germs, saving lives : the quest
for the first vaccines / by Glen Phelan.
p. cm.— (Science quest)
Trade ISBN: 0-7922-5537-2
Library Edition ISBN: 0-7922-5538-0
Includes bibliographical
references and index.
1. Vaccines—History—Juvenile
literature. I. Title. II. Science quest
(National Geographic Society (U.S.))
QR189.P454 2006
615'.372'09—dc22
                        2005022143

**PUBLISHED BY THE
NATIONAL GEOGRAPHIC SOCIETY**

John M. Fahey, Jr.,
President and Chief Executive Officer

Gilbert M. Grosvenor,
Chairman of the Board

Nina D. Hoffman,
*Executive Vice President, President of
Books & Education Publishing Group*

Ericka Markman, *Senior Vice President,
President of Children's Books & Education
Publishing Group*

Steve Mico, *Senior Vice President &
Publisher of Children's Books and
Education Publishing Group*

Bea Jackson, *Design Director, Children's
Books & Education Publishing Group*

**PREPARED BY NATIONAL GEOGRAPHIC
CHILDREN'S BOOKS**

Nancy Laties Feresten, *Vice President,
Editor-in-Chief of Children's Books*

Jim Hiscott, *Art Director, Children's Books
& Education Publishing Group*

Susan Kehnemui Donnelly,
Project Editor

KINETIK, *Designer*

Lori Epstein, *Illustrations Editor*

Jean Cantu, *Illustrations Coordinator*

R. Gary Colbert, *Production Director*

Lewis R. Bassford, *Production Manager*

Vincent P. Ryan, *Manufacturing Manager*

**PROGRAM DEVELOPMENT FOR
NATIONAL GEOGRAPHIC READING
EXPEDITIONS**
Kate Boehm Jerome

CONSULTANT/REVIEWERS
Dr. James Shymansky, E. Desmond
Lee Professor of Science Education,
University of Missouri-St. Louis

Photo credits-Cover, © Bettmann/Corbis;
4, National Library of Medicine; 6,
Juergen Berger/Max-Planck
Institute/Photo Researchers, Inc.; 8-9,
NIBSC/Science Photo Library/Photo
Researchers, Inc.; 10, Bridgeman Art
Library; 12-13, Hulton Archive/Getty
Images; 14, © Bettmann/Corbis; 15, ©
Archivo Iconografico, S.A./Corbis; 16, ©
Markow Tatiana/Corbis Sygma; 17, ©
Archivo Iconografico, S.A. /Corbis; 18, ©
Bettmann/Corbis; 19, © Stephanie
Maze/Corbis; 20, © Bettmann/Corbis; 21,
Musée Pasteur/Institut Pasteur-Paris; 22-
23, © Hulton-Deutsch Collection /Corbis;
24 (l), Science Photo Library/Photo
Researchers, Inc.; (r), Taxi/Getty Images;
25, © Bettmann/Corbis; 26 (l), © Corbis;
26 (r), Taxi/Getty Images; 27, Yale
Joel/Time & Life Pictures/Getty Images;
28-29, The Granger Collection, New York;
30, © Stapleton Collection/Corbis; 31, ©
Bettmann/Corbis; 32 (l), © Bettmann/
Corbis; 32 (r), Ryan McVay/Getty Images;
33, © Bettmann/Corbis; 34-35, ©
Michael Boys/Corbis; 36, © AFP /Corbis;
37, The Granger Collection, New York; 38,
Musée Pasteur/Institut Pasteur-Paris; 39,
Chris Bjornberg/Photo Researchers, Inc.;
40-41, © Charles O'Rear/Corbis; 42,
National Library of Medicine; 43, ©
Bettmann/Corbis; 44, Musée Pasteur/Institut
Pasteur-Paris; 45, © Bettmann/Corbis;
46-47, © Bettmann/Corbis; 48, Science
Photo Library/Photo Researchers, Inc.;
49, National Library of Medicine/Science
Photo Library/Photo Researchers, Inc.; 50,
NASA; 51, © Tom Stewart/Corbis; 52, Jonas
Salk Stamp Design © 1998 United States
Postal Service. Used with permission. All
rights reserved; 53, © Reuters/Corbis; 54-
55, Tek Image/Science Photo Library/Photo
Researchers, Inc.; 56, © Lester V. Bergman/
Corbis; 58, © Lester Lefkowitz/Corbis.

One of the world's largest nonprofit scientific and educational organizations, the
National Geographic Society was founded
in 1888 "for the increase and diffusion of
geographic knowledge." Fulfilling this
mission, the Society educates and inspires
millions every day through its magazines,
books, television programs, videos, maps
and atlases, research grants, the National
Geographic Bee, teacher workshops, and
innovative classroom materials. The Society
is supported through membership dues,
charitable gifts, and income from the sale
of its educational products. This support is
vital to National Geographic's mission to
increase global understanding and promote
conservation of our planet through explo-
ration, research, and education.

For more information, please call

1-800-NGS-LINE (647-5463)
or write to the following address:

NATIONAL GEOGRAPHIC SOCIETY
1145 17th Street N.W.
Washington, D.C. 20036-4688
U.S.A.

Visit the Society's Web site:
www.nationalgeographic.com

Printed in Belgium.